HOW TO NETWORK FOR BUSINESS SUCCESS

Grow Your Business Profits

© 2018 mcHoward Business Coaching **ALL RIGHTS RESERVED.**

No part of this book may be reproduced or transmitted in any form whatsoever, electronic, or mechanical, including photocopying, recording, or by any informational storage or retrieval system without the expressed written, dated and signed permission from the authors.

Published by:

mcHoward Business Coaching
203 S Stratford Rd Ste T
Winston-Salem, NC 27103

LIMITS OF LIABILITY / DISCLAIMER OF WARRANTY:

The authors and publisher of this book have used their best efforts in preparing this material. While every attempt has been made to verify information provided in this book, neither the authors nor the publisher assumes any responsibility for any errors, omissions or inaccuracies.

The authors and publisher make no representation or warranties with respect to the accuracy, applicability, fitness, or completeness of the contents of this program. They disclaim any warranties (expressed or implied), merchantability, or fitness for any purpose. The authors and publisher shall in no event be held liable for any loss or other damages, including but not limited to special, incidental, consequential, or other damages. As always, the advice of a competent legal, tax, accounting or other professional should be sought.

How to Network for Business Success

The purpose of this book is to walk you through a process we've created where you can use networking to grow your business!

We will go through 10 simple strategies that you can use which will help you get the results you need when you are networking. Most people know nothing about these strategies, and therefore are failing to capitalize on their revenue-generating power.

For the purposes of this book, we'll cover each of the 10 strategies in individual chapters… for one main reason. We want you to be able to review these strategies and minimize the amount of time it will take you to implement them in their entirety.

However, consider this… people network because they do not have money to advertise. And, just as with advertising, your networking should involve a well-crafted message that compels anyone you share it with, to want to know more. You also must have a business card that supports your message. Your business card is the invitation for whoever you are speaking with to learn more.

As a business owner or entrepreneur, if you're struggling right now to generate more leads and clients through networking, and you need to maximize your time and grow your revenue and profits, then spend the next few minutes with us and we'll show you how we can help you make all these problems disappear forever.

Small business owners today are desperate for proven and tested ways they can generate more leads, attract more clients and make more money. So, what if we told you that we can show you how to generate all the leads a business owner needs - through networking? Networking for your business is not a social activity. You network for one reason - to grow your business.

Over the next few minutes, we're going to give you back door access to a series of powerful networking strategies which are some of the most powerful revenue-generating strategies ever created.

So, let's get started.

Chapter 1

Starting the Networking Conversation

The most difficult thing to do when networking is to start a networking conversation. The difficulty comes, because we walk into a networking event looking to get business; that is how we are wired. You must change your mindset and behavior from an inward focus to an outward focus. Remember, no one came to the networking event to buy anything.

When you meet someone you should ask, "What do you do and what is the biggest challenge or issue you are currently facing?" One of the 10 business fundamentals of human behavior you must remember when you market your business, is that people want to buy from a business that is unique. Again, no one came to buy, but asking this question will make you and your business memorable and unique. This question will compel the person with whom you are talking to be open and share.

When we are coaching leaders, we coach them on how to communicate seven different ways. Each of the seven ways to communicate and the communication strategies guide the leader on what they need say in any situation they may encounter. We also teach them how to listen. When networking, you will need to master the art of listening - to help the person you just met. When you ask the question, what do you do, and what is the biggest challenge or issue you are currently facing, how you listen will strongly impact the results you achieve when networking.

Chapter 2

How to Purposefully Listen to Maximize Your Results

There are many ways to purposefully listen, but we will only identify a few that you need to master when you are networking. One listening strategy you can execute is to listen to help. Here, you are listening for a way to help who you just met overcome a problem they may be experiencing. This problem does not necessarily have to be with their business. Their problem could be that their air conditioning is not working and they do not know a reputable HVAC company to call to fix it. If you have an HVAC company in your network that you can refer them to, this person will be forever grateful, and therefore, will want to help you. You can call the HVAC company you referred after they complete the job. Find out if everything worked out. If things went well and he/she was paid for the referral you just gave, you can now request help getting what you need…a referral. Actually, you have positioned yourself to get a referral from the two people you just helped.

Another listening strategy is listening for priorities. After asking the networking question, "What do you do, and what is the biggest challenge or issue you are currently facing?" listen for things that appear to be important to the person you just met. Perhaps a priority is becoming debt free, improving their credit score because they are applying for a loan, or getting their child prepared to be admitted to college. While this is not a problem, it is a priority for this person. We might say to them, "I know someone who specializes in all of those things. Dr. Andrea Johnson with ANJ Consulting has helped many people successfully navigate those areas. Would you like me to introduce you to Dr. Andrea?

Sometimes, you will hear individuals share that they need an opportunity. Listening for an opportunity will position you to connect the person to another person who can offer them an opportunity, such as a job or an opportunity to volunteer. Listening for emotion is another way you can position yourself to be unique and valuable to the person you just met. Perhaps, after answering the networking question, they expressed excitement about a new account he/she just landed. You see that they are excited about the great work they just completed! Maybe you know someone in the same industry within your network who could benefit from an introduction to this individual. How do you think they will feel about you for creating yet another opportunity?

These are just a few ways in which you can position yourself to help someone you just met while networking. These listening strategies will evoke so much emotion in the individual, that if you need an introduction or a donation from the Pope, they will feel compelled to introduce you to someone who is one to three phone calls away from the person or target for which you need an introduction.

Chapter 3

The Networking Conversation

A referral target is someone who works in an industry. For example, HR Directors, Executive Directors, Book Keepers and Commercial Insurance Agents are good targets for us. We have discovered with various networking groups we have started; most networkers have not taken the time to determine who is a good target for them. You may have to ask them coaching questions to help them determine who is already doing business with their potential clients. You must also know who your own target is when they ask you. We will cover that in the next chapter.

The key to success here is to ask the networking question and then select a listening strategy and get them connected.

Ask > Listen > Connect

Ask: Hello, I am _____ what do you do and what is the biggest challenge or issue you are currently facing?

Listen: Select one of the listening strategies to ensure you are purposefully listening. (This is the most important part of this sequence necessary to maximize your networking results)

Connect: Identify who in your network you can connect them to who will help them overcome their issue and create emotion to compel them to want to do the same for you.

We promise, by executing this networking sequence you will develop deeper business and personal relationships. And, you will create a valuable network of people who will help you grow your business/career to levels you could never achieve on your own.

This is your formula to networking success. Memorize it...practice it...own it!

Chapter 4

Now You Must Share Who Is Your Target

Many businesses can't answer the question: *Who is your target market?* They have often made the fatal assumption that *everyone* will want to purchase their product or service with the right marketing strategy.

A target market is simply the group of customers or clients who will purchase a specific product or service. This group of people all have something in common, often age, gender, hobbies, or location.

Your target market then, is the people who will buy your offering. This includes both existing and potential customers, all of whom are motivated to do one of three things:
- Fulfill a need
- Solve a problem
- Satisfy a desire

To build, maintain, and grow your business, you need to know who your customers are, what they do, what they like, and why they would buy your product or service. Getting this wrong – or not taking the time to get it right – will cost you time, money, and potentially the success of your business.

The Importance of Knowing Your Target Market

Knowledge and understanding of your target market is the keystone in the arch of your business. Without it, your product or service positioning, pricing, marketing strategy and eventually, your business could very quickly fall apart.

If you don't intimately know your target market, you run the risk of making mistakes when it comes to establishing pricing, product mix, or service packages. Your marketing strategy will lack direction, and produce mediocre results at best. Even if your marketing message and unique selling proposition (USP) are clear and your brochure is perfectly designed, it means nothing unless it arrives in the hands (or ears) of the right people.

Determining your target market takes time and careful diligence. While it often starts with a best guess, assumptions cannot be relied on and research is required to confirm original ideas. Your target market is not always your ideal market.

Once you build an understanding of who your target market is, keep up with your market research. Having your finger on the pulse of their motivations and drivers – which naturally change – will help you to anticipate needs or wants and evolve your business.

Types of Markets

Consumer

The Consumer Market includes those general consumers who buy products and services for personal use, or for use by family and friends. This is the market category you or I fall into when we're shopping for groceries or clothes, seeing a movie in the theatre, or going out for lunch. Retailers focus on this market category when marketing their goods or services.

Institutional

The Institutional Market serves society and provides products or services for the benefit of society. This includes hospitals, non-profit organizations, government organizations, schools and universities. Members of the Institutional Market purchase products to use in the provision of services to people in their care.

Business to Business (B2B)

The B2B Market is just what it seems to be: businesses that purchase the products and services of other businesses - to run their operations. These purchases can include products which are used to manufacture other products (raw or technical), products which are needed for daily operations (such as office supplies), or services (such as accounting, shredding, and legal).

Reseller

This market can also be called the "Intermediary Market" because it consists of businesses that act as channels for goods and services between other markets. Goods are purchased and sold for a profit – without any alterations. Members of this market include wholesalers, retailers, resellers, and distributors.

Determining Your Target Market

Product / Service Investigation

The process for determining your target market starts by examining exactly what your offering is, and what the average customer's motivation for purchasing it is. Start by answering the following questions:

Does your offering meet a basic need?	
Does your offering serve a particular want?	
Does your offering fulfill a desire?	
What is the lifecycle of your product / service?	

What is the availability of your offering?	
What is the cost of the average customer's purchase?	
What is the lifecycle of your offering?	
How many times or how often will customers purchase your offering?	
Do you foresee any upcoming changes in your industry or region that may affect the sale of your offering (positive/negative)?	

Market Investigation

- **On the ground.** Spend some time on the ground researching who your target market might be. If you're thinking about opening a coffee shop, hang out in the neighborhood at different times of the day to get a sense of the people who live, work, and play in the neighborhood. Notice their age, gender, clothing, and any other indications of income and activities.

- **At the competition.** Who is your direct competitor targeting? Is there a small niche that is being missed? Observing the clientele of your competition can help to build understanding of your target market, regardless of whether it is the same or opposite. For example, if you own a children's clothing boutique and the majority of middle-class mothers shop at the local department store, you may wish to focus on higher-income families as your target market.

- **Online.** Many cities and towns – or at least regions – have demographic information available online. Research the ages, incomes, occupations, and other key pieces of information about the people who live in the area you operate your business. From this data, you will gain an understanding of the size of your total potential market.

- **With existing customers.** Talk to your existing customers through focus groups or surveys. This is a great way to gather demographic and behavioral information, as well as genuine feedback about product or service quality and other information which will be useful in a business or marketing strategy.

Who is Your Market?

Based on your product / service and market investigations, you will be able to piece together a basic picture of your target market, and some of their general characteristics. Record some notes here. At this point, you may wish to be as specific as possible, or maintain some generalities. You can further segment your market in the next section.

Target Market Sample 1: Consumer Market

Business: Baby Clothing Boutique	**Business Purpose:** *Meet a need* (provide clothing for infants and children aged 0 to 5 years) *Serve a want* (clothing is brand name only, and has a higher price point than the competition)
Market Type: Consumer	
Gender: Women	
Marital Status: Married	
Market Observations: Located on Main Street of Anytown, a street that is seeing many new boutiques open up, proximate to the main shopping mall two blocks from popular mid-range restaurant that is busy at lunch	**Industry Predictions:** Large number of new housing developments in the city and surrounding areas Two new schools in construction expect to see an influx of new families move to town from Anycity
Competition Observations: Baby clothing also available at two local department stores, and one second-hand shop on opposite side of town	**Online Research:** Half of Anytown's population is female, and 25% have children under the age of 15 years Anytown's population is expected to increase by 32% within three years The average household income for Anytown is $75,000 annually

TARGET MARKET: The target market can then be described as married mothers with children under five years old, between the ages of 25 and 45, who have recently moved to Anytown from Anycity, and have a household income of at least $100K annually.

If your business is B2C complete the chart on the following page.

Consumer Target Market Framework

Market Type:	Consumer
Gender:	☐ Male ☐ Female
Age Range:	
Purchase Motivation:	☐ Meet a Need ☐ Serve a Want ☐ Fulfill a Desire
Activities:	
Income Range:	
Marital Status:	
Location:	☐ Neighborhood ☐ City ☐ Region ☐ Country
Other Notes:	

Institutional Target Market Framework

Market Type:	Institutional
Institution Type:	☐ Hospital ☐ Non-profit ☐ School ☐ University ☐ Charity ☐ Government ☐ Church
Purchase Motivation:	☐ Operational Need ☐ Client Want ☐ Client Desire
Purpose of Institution:	
Institution's Client Base:	
Size:	
Location:	☐ Neighborhood ☐ City ☐ Region ☐ Country
Other Notes:	

Target Market Sample 2: B2B Market

Business: Confidential Paper Shredding	**Target Business Size:** Small to medium
Market Type: B2B (Business to Business)	**Target Business Revenue:** $500K to $1M
Business Purpose: *Meet an operations need* (provide confidential on-site shredding services for business documents)	**Target Business Type:** Produce or handle a variety of sensitive paper documentation Accountants, lawyers, real estate agents, etc.
Market Observations: There are two main areas of office buildings and industrial warehouses in Anycity Three more office towers are being constructed, and will be completed this year	**Industry Predictions:** The professional sector is seeing revenue growth of 24% over last year, which indicates increased client billing and staff recruitment
Competition Observations: One confidential shredding company serves the region, covering Anycity and the surrounding towns Provide regular (weekly or biweekly) service, but does not have the capacity to handle large volumes at one time	**Online Research:** Anycity's biggest employment sectors are: manufacturing, tourism, food services, and professional services

TARGET MARKET:

The target market can then be described as small to medium sized businesses in the professional sector with an annual revenue of $500K to $1M who require both regular and infrequent large volume paper shredding services.

If your business is B2B complete the chart on the next page.

B2B Target Market Framework

Market Type:	Business to Business (B2B)
Company Size:	
Number of Employees:	
Purchase Motivation:	☐ Operations Need ☐ Strategy ☐ Functionality
Annual Revenue:	
Industry:	
Location(s):	
Purpose of Business:	
People, Culture & Values:	
Other Notes:	

Your Target Market: Putting It Together

Based on the information you gather from your product / service and market investigations, you should have a clear vision of your realistic target market. Here are a few examples of how this information is put together and conclusions are drawn:

Segmenting Your Market

Your market segments are the groups within your target market – broken down by a determinant in one of the following four categories:
- Demographics
- Psychographics
- Geographics
- Behaviors

Segmenting your target market into several more specific groups allows you to further tailor your marketing campaign and more specifically position your product or service. You may wish to divide your marketing campaign into four sections, and target four specific markets with messages that will most resonate with the audience.

For example, the baby clothing store may choose to segment its target market by psychographics, or lifestyle. If the larger target market is *married females with children under five, between the ages of 25 and 45, who have a household income of at least $100K annually*, it can be broken down into the following lifestyle segments:
- Fitness-oriented mothers
- Career-oriented mothers
- New mothers

With these three categories, unique marketing messages can be created that speak to the hot-buttons of each segment. The more accurate and specific you can make communications with your target market, the greater impact you will have on your revenues.

Market Segmentation Variables

Demographic	Psychographic	Geographic	Behavioristic
Age Income Gender Generation Nationality Ethnicity Marital Status Family Size Occupation Religion Language Education Employment Type Housing Type Housing Ownership Political Affiliation	Personality Lifestyle Values Attitude Motivation Activities Interests	Region Country City Area Neighborhood Density Climate	Brand Loyalty Product Usage Purchase Frequency Profitability Readiness to Buy User Status

Understanding Your Target Market

Once you have determined who your market is, make a point of learning everything you can about them. You need to have a strong understanding of who they are, what they like, where they shop, why they buy, and how they spend their time. Remind yourself that you may *think* you know your market, but until you have verified the information, you'll be driving your marketing strategy blind.

Also, be aware that markets change, just like people. Just because you knew your market when you started your business 5 or 10 years ago, doesn't mean that you know it now. Regular market research is part of any successful business plan, and a great habit to start. If you don't believe us, ask Toys R Us or any other brick-and-mortar retailer.

Chapter 5

Your Business Card

- **Cover the basics.** A business card needs to communicate your basic contact information to potential clients, including who you are and *what your business does*. Make sure you've covered the basics and made it easy for them to get in touch with you. You should use a headline on your business card to get your prospect's attention. Use the back of the card to provide a low risk offer.

   > **Company name**
   > **Name**
   > **Title**
   > **Hot Button Headline**
   > **Website or landing page**
   > **Email**
   > **Phone**
   > **Cell Phone (if applicable)**
   > **Social media URLs**
   > **A low risk offer on the reverse side**

- **Make it memorable. Be creative.** Choose interesting shapes, die-cuts, orientation (vertical vs. horizontal), bright colors, and unique materials (wood, plastic, magnet, aluminum or foam). You don't have to go crazy or spend lots of money to do this –

simple, clever twists on basic design make an impact. Just keep it relevant to your product or service.

- **Give them a reason to keep it.** What is going to keep them from throwing it out, or filing it in a 3" binder of other cards? Make the card worth keeping by adding something useful to the backside. For example, coffee shops put frequent buyer incentives on the backside of their cards, encouraging customers to keep them in their wallets. Other examples include: pick-up schedules, reminders, calendars, testimonials, or coupons.

- **Produce a high quality card.** Use at least 100lb card stock, and print in color. Choose clear, easy to read fonts that aren't any smaller than 9pt.

Your business card acts as a small flyer to support everything you have shared that you do for your target market. Your headline should speak to the problem your prospect is having in their head. Your offer should be your prospect's pathway to solving the problem.

Chapter 6

The Event

If you execute the strategies and tactics we have shared here consistently, you will be successful. We can tell you that most people you will encounter while networking will do it wrong. If you execute one of the networking strategies we have shared - you will have limited success; however, if you implement everything we have share here, the sky is the limit! There is one last thing to consider...your audience and knowing who is in the room.

What do we mean by audience and knowing who is in the room? Once you know who is in the room, that will determine which elevator pitch you will use. For instance, if we were at a corporate event, and we were asked, "What do you do?" - We would share – "We show leaders how to avoid being one-trick ponies when they communicate with their teams. This helps the leader improve engagement of the team and lower turnover."

If we were attending a Chamber Event, we would share - "I am a Business Breakthrough Strategist. I can turn any businesses around in 45 minutes or less. The tactics I cover with business owners usually show them where at least $10,000 is hidden in their business."

Ultimately, you will have more than one elevator pitch. If we were attending an event with realtors at the Realtor Association, we might share – "I help new home owners get the cash they need to buy furniture, appliances or decor for their new home. I can usually let them know within 60 seconds if they are approved and they won't have a hard pull on their credit."

Do you see what we are doing here?

We have prepared elevator pitches for any networking event we might attend. The fact that we do more than one thing and we have more than one pitch helps us to avoid sounding like a me-too business, if a similar business is in the room.

Coach Antonio: "In one of our Infinity Strategic Partners networking groups a fellow was invited who does some of the things I do when it comes to business growth; specifically social media marketing. He asked for introductions to restaurant owners. What he does for restaurants, I can do as well. He gave his 60 second elevator pitch when his turn came. I thought, "I need to speak about something else, so he can refer to me and everyone else is not confused and think we both do the same thing." Since his target was restaurants, I spoke about how I help struggling restaurant owners capture the email addresses of all of their customers, so they can market to those customers for repeat business and grow profits. I was able to do that, because I had developed an elevator pitch earlier for this service. I had to pull from the elevator pitch library in my brain and use the one I have for Social WiFi. By the way, that visitor who offered the same services I did gave me a referral, because he did not offer Social WiFi." How cool is that?!?

Our point here is that you need to develop more than one elevator pitch, based on who is in the room. We shared one example where you may attend different events and you need to have a pitch for each event, simply because the audience probably will not be the same. We also shared an example of how you may need a different pitch based on an the example of a networking group where someone gives their 60 second pitch before you and you are both in the same business. You will have to have a different 60 second elevator pitch ready within minutes, in order to educate the partners in group, and ultimately get a referral.

Remember this…

Be especially certain that your introduction will also roll off the tongue of the person who may be able to refer to you. Imagine the embarrassment of your strategic partner recognizing a referral for you, and they struggle with your introduction. "You need to meet Bob Jones with Acme Industrial………um……. something….um." It would not be their fault, especially if you made your introduction complicated in an effort to impress.

One last thing about your elevator pitch: It should roll off your tongue like your name. You shouldn't be stumbling and looking in the air trying to find the words to explain to someone what you do. If you don't sound polished when you give your pitch, you will sound as though you don't have confidence. People do not refer to nor spend money with people who do not have confidence.

Practice…Practice…Practice…

Chapter 7

How to Develop Your Elevator Pitch

Developing an elevator pitch requires a certain level of skill. By that we mean: you must be able to identify some things before you develop it. Who is the target you solve the problem for? What emotion are they experiencing when they have this problem? It may be frustration, overwhelm, fear or are they anxious, happy etc...

You will also need to express what they are feeling after you have implemented your solution and they no longer have the problem.

Look at the template below to see the process you should go through to create your 60 second elevator pitch.

(I / We) (action verb - help, guide, teach, review, provide, consult with, present, aid, assist, support, grant, give, award, evaluate, assess)
(negative emotions being experienced - frustrated, furious, overwhelmed, clueless, demanding, frightened, desperate, struggling, angry, concerned, worried)
(ideal client description - dog lovers, young adults, chronic pain sufferers, overweight men, homeowners, business owners, brides-to-be, new mothers)
who want to (what they want - increase their profits, find an honest plumber, purchase that perfect diamond, find the relief they need, find the best deal)

(solution - discover a process, learn a fast and easy way, create the perfect solution, uncover the best method, determine the number one reason, realize the best course of action, find the dramatic solution, locate the best deal, position themselves, place themselves first, find out everything they need to know)
to / so that they can (list 3 benefits - live a pain free life, build the business of their dreams, finally give the perfect gift, feel they're getting the most value for the money they pay, pay the lowest price, receive the highest value, obtain the best guarantee, receive award-winning service, receive the highest level of expertise at the lowest possible price).

As you can see, this is simple. Take some time and craft a few elevator pitches on the next page for different audiences based on the template.

One Audience

I am _____ WITH _____. I (help, consult, assist)

(Your target) _ (mothers, business owners, teachers)_____

_____(with this problem)_____

_____.

A (mothers, business owner, teacher) _____WAS REFERRED TO ME BECAUSE (what problem did they have?)_____

_____

_____,

AND NOW (since they met with you)

_____
_____.

THIS WEEK I WOULD LIKE AN INTRODUCTION TO
(NAME)_____,
(TITLE)_____
(PROFESSION)_____.

_____

(Your Tag line)

Another Audience

I am _____ WITH _____. I (help, consult, assist)

(Your target) _ (mothers, business owners, teachers)_____

_____(with this problem)_____

_____.

A (mother business owner, teacher) _____WAS REFERRED TO ME BECAUSE (what problem did they have?)_____

_____

_____, AND NOW (since they met with you)

_____
_____.

THIS WEEK I WOULD LIKE AN INTRODUCTION TO
(NAME)_____,
(TITLE)_____
(PROFESSION)_____.

_____

(Your Tag line)

Chapter 8

How You Should Follow Up

If you are like us and you have done plenty of networking, you have a stack of business cards from all of the events you have attended. The sad part about the stack of business cards is that you have not looked at them again since the event. You are missing an opportunity by not acting on the business cards you have received. Before you wig out on us, because you think we are going to ask you to call everyone in your stack of business cards; relax. We have something more strategic in mind. Take out the business cards and put them in piles. Organize the stack into those people who are acquaintances and those who could possibly already be doing business with your potential clients.

The stack of business cards you have for industries that are already doing business with your prospective clients are your most important cards. Connect with these individuals on LinkedIn and use the private messenger feature to see if you can have coffee or a phone call. For the other stack, connect on LinkedIn, but do not set an appointment to have coffee or a call. We must manage our time wisely, and this can get out of hand quickly if not managed properly. You will be connecting with these individuals only as connection partners when you need them to help you connect with someone you need to meet, that you do not yet know.

For us - we would create a pile for insurance agents, web developers, HR people, accountants, tailors and merchant service providers. We could add more, but we will stop here. These people are doing business with business owners and executives. The HR people and the tailors are doing business with executives and the other professions previously listed are doing business with business owners (our potential clients). We would connect, and we would send this message using the private message function:

"Hello John/Jane, it was great meeting at the Venture Cafe event last night. I would like to grab some coffee to learn more about what you do and explore how we can help each other grow our businesses. What are a couple of days/times that you have available next week?

When you get to the coffee shop, just like in the networking meeting - focus on how you can help them. One strategy we teach executive coaching clients to use when they have been passed over for promotion is to ask for advice. We train our clients to reach out and connect with high-level executives by asking them for advice. This creates some visibility to advance our client's career, not to mention it begins a relationship with a high-level executive who probably has influence. You must start the conversation by asking the individual for advice on how to solve the problem you are having. This builds trust quickly because the message you are sending to this individual is: "I trust you and I value your opinion." For the executive we are coaching, it gives them much needed visibility with this high-level individual. We would also ask to connect with them on LinkedIn.

Going forward, whenever you connect with an individual at any event...even church and family events, connect with them on

LinkedIn within 24 hours of receiving the business card or meeting them. If it is a family event or church and business cards are not being exchanged, jot their name down on the note pad app on your smart phone, and connect with them on LinkedIn when you get home. The 24-hour time frame is important because you want to do this while your name and face are fresh in their minds. This gives them a chance to really learn about you and you can do the same with them. LinkedIn is a valuable tool when doing face-to-face networking.

LinkedIn is also the place where you can create massive visibility about what you do. When we conduct conflict resolution workshops or leadership retreats, we post the pictures on LinkedIn with a little text to let our network know, this is what we do. Our professional network, family and friends get to see that a company contracted with us to do this work, and that says we are respected thought leaders in this space. This will attract others in our network to reach out and inquire about hiring us for future opportunities. You can do this, too.

LinkedIn is an integral part of your networking strategy. LinkedIn gives you a place to let your network know who you are and what value you bring to the market place. If your LinkedIn profile does share what problem you solve and for whom - reach out us - we can help you get it there.

Chapter 9

Your LinkedIn Profile

LinkedIn is the largest professional network on the web. Unlike Facebook, your persona on LinkedIn should be professional. This platform contains recruiters and high-level executives. Your profile is important, and it must convey an accurate image of you. We recommend getting a professional headshot. Montinique Cager at FAO Studios can do your headshot and he does excellent work.

The next thing that must be addressed is your headline. Most people put their current position in their headline. We believe these individuals are missing opportunities to show how they add value to the market place or other organizations. At one time, we wanted to attract leaders who were dealing with conflict on their teams. Our headline read:

Helping leaders resolve conflict and raise productivity and lower turnover

Our current headline reads:

Need to generate more leads, close more sales, and increase revenue and profits?

Do you have any idea who we are trying to attract with this headline? Is there any question about what value we bring to the market place?

Your headline should do this work for you.

You should have an engaging cover photo that reinforces your brand through colors and you should use appropriate images to make people want to learn more and continue reading through your profile.

Your summary should further explain what you do and what problem you solve and for whom. We recommend writing in the third-party, which is an easy way to add credibility. It should be key word rich, so as to make your profile searchable. You can also indicate a call-to-action and even make an offer.

Add skills you do well to your profile and indicate your education. Share your causes that you volunteer for and positions that you served in while advancing these causes. Your profile should give those who view it a glimpse of who you are, how you have developed yourself, and how you choose to give back.

What LinkedIn does better than any other social media platform is show you who your network knows. You can then reach out the person you are connected to and share who you need to meet. Therefore, we suggest you connect with everyone you meet, because LinkedIn will tell you who your contacts may know. Then, your call is to your contact to get an introduction.

When coaching leaders, we share that we are gradually moving into a career environment where resumes are becoming obsolete. More advanced companies are asking for a copy of your LinkedIn profile. Would you be proud to send yours? Would your profile do the work needed to create a new opportunity?

Chapter 10
Start Your Own Networking Group

We have spent the last 9 chapters discussing what you need to do to navigate the networking environment, so that you can achieve massive success and drive results for your business. We have also talked about networking groups. Networking groups like a Chamber leads group is where you will stand up and give a 60 second elevator pitch about the introductions you need. These groups are great to visit; however, there is a slim chance you will get the introductions you need. There is another option - Starting your own group!

This may seem like a daunting task, yet it is easier than you may think. Most people build a networking group by having certain categories or industries in their group. That may work, but it is also a bit limiting. What would you say if we told you the category does not matter? The only thing that matters is that you have people in the room who want to help you first, before receiving a referral from you. The quality of the people in the room matters more than anything else.

We have started networking groups where we had 2 realtors, 2 mortgage lenders, 2 financial advisors, and 3 attorneys. What made these industry overlaps work, was that each person was concerned with what their partner needed. They could connect their partner to whom ever they requested through their cell phone contacts or social media connections. This group was fun, to say the least! There was really no chapter within our organization whose category profile resembled ours.

In order to start a group, all you need is 8-10 people you know who would like to help you and help others grow their businesses. We typically see an insurance person, a realtor, a mortgage lender, an HVAC company, a pest control company, a web developer, a financial advisor, and a business consultant in a group. These professions can agree to meet weekly - specifically to be connected to the individuals they need to meet.

What we have seen work is; the fewer people the better. These results happen when you use the Infinity Strategic Partners framework. We have seen no less than 10 referrals per week. If you have an interest in having your own group, please reach out to us. This is a money-making business opportunity. Another benefit of having your own group is that you get to decide who you are networking with regularly. We have started six groups and it has been very rewarding for us to help other business owners reach their goals, not to mention the financial benefit of our own businesses.

The only thing standing in your way now is getting all of this implemented in a timely and efficient manner. Please let us know if this is something you would like us to help you with! We are available for consulting and speaking. Connect with us on LinkedIn or Facebook, and you can always text or give us a call.

Glen Coleman 336-756-2205 & Antonio McCoy 336-575-9920

www.ingramcontent.com/pod-product-compliance
Lightning Source LLC
Chambersburg PA
CBHW030102230526
45471CB00003B/1209